Self-portrait, 1634
Oil on canvas,
55 x 46cm
Copenhagen,
National Art Museum

MATISSE

"I have worked to enrich my knowledge, satisfying the diverse curiosities of my mind, striving to discover the different thoughts of the ancient and the modern masters of form."
Henri Matisse 1907

Henri Matisse, painter, sculptor, draughtsman, book illustrator and - at the very end of his life - architect, was born at Le Cateau in northern France on 31 December 1869. His father was a chemist and grain-merchant, his mother came from a long line of glove-makers. There was nothing in this solid commercial background to suggest any latent artistic brilliance; Matisse, indeed, retained a commercial sharpness throughout his life as art dealers found to their cost. This was unusual for an artist who, with Picasso, has come to be regarded as the greatest painter of the 20th century. His early life was anything but brilliant, however.

Matisse attended the lycée at Saint Quentin before going up to Paris for his law exams in 1888, without showing any artistic interests; he did not even visit the Louvre on this first stay in Paris. Then, recovering from appendicitis in 1890, he was given a box of paints to dabble with. Suddenly, he seems to have discovered an overriding passion to become a painter. From then on, despite many setbacks in early years, and intermittent grave doubts about his own real abilities, he worked determinedly at his chosen course.

He sat but failed the entrance exams for the famous Ecole des Beaux Arts in Paris but was accepted into the studio of Gustave Moreau, the Symbolist painter, in 1895. Moreau, whose own paintings are today not greatly admired, was a sympathetic and generous teacher. In his studios Matisse met artists who became lifelong friends, such as Georges Rouault and Albert Marquet; he also received a firm grounding in the academic art he was soon to reject so fiercely, and copied as an exercise various famous works like Chardin's *The Ray.*

But it was a more original work, *Woman Reading,* which first won him acclaim in 1896, being purchased for the nation. Significantly, this quiet domestic interior pointed to some of his future themes - idyllic domestic scenes. He was then accepted into the fairly conservative Salon du Champ-de-Mars, a semi-official body; Matisse seemed destined to become a financially successful, quietly conservative painter, affluent enough to be able to support a wife and family.

This factor must have been important to him, for he was never a

Matisse photographed in his studio at Issy-les-Moulineaux in 1909

frequenter of bars or cafes, preferring domestic quiet attended by devoted women. He had fallen in love with Amelie Parayre, who bore him a daughter in 1894. They could not afford to marry until 1898; then, on the advice of the Impressionist Pissaro, they decided to spend their honeymoon in London, where Matisse admired Turner's works.

In 1896 Matisse had met the painter John Russell who introduced him to the works of Van Gogh and the Impressionists. Matisse reacted only cautiously to these strong influences, which many of his friends had already absorbed. Far greater was the impact of Cézanne's work, which Matisse first saw at Vollard's gallery in 1895. At great financial sacrifice (reputedly selling his wife's engagement ring) he bought Cézanne's *The Three Bathers* in 1899; Matisse saw Cézanne as an ideal of the artist who had struggled in near-isolation to achieve his mature greatness. Inspired by his example, Matisse began to paint in a more original but much less popular way.

The first years of the century were grim ones for Matisse. Both his wife's and his own health suffered from their poverty and he was forced to rely on the generosity of his parents; he opened a small art school to supplement his income and contemplated abandoning painting altogether. But his first one-man exhibition with the influential art dealer Vollard in 1904 attracted reasonable reviews and his sales slowly began to improve.

In the same year Matisse and his family spent the summer at Saint Tropez with Signac, the leader of the Post-Impressionists. Here he painted *Luxe, Calme Et Volupté* - a painting brimming with the south's colours and so much in the Pointillist manner that Signac, delighted, bought it at once. But Post-Impressionism, for all its vibrant colours, could not hold Matisse for long. The posthumous influence of Gauguin, growing with exhibitions in 1903, 1904 and 1905, now began to exert its lasting power over him. After his purchase of a

Cézanne, Matisse bought a painting by Gauguin. He also began sculpting at this time, under the influence of Rodin and African sculptures.

On 18 October 1905 an exhibition of works by Matisse and similar artists like Maurice Vlaminck and André Derain, opened at the Salon d'Automne in Paris. Entering, the critic Louis Vauxcelles spotted a classical bust among the (to him) lurid canvases and cried out: "Look, Donatello (a Renaissance sculptor) among the wild beasts (les Fauves)!" The name Fauvist stuck although Matisse always disliked the term. Compared either to smooth academic art or the calm light displays of Impressionism, works like *Joie De*

Matisse with his sculpture The Serpentine Woman *finished in 1909*

Vivre (Joy Of Life, page 4) or *Portrait With The Green Stripe* (page 6) were indeed wild in their strident colours. Public reaction was vehemently hostile; Matisse was taken aback but soon realised that any publicity at all was welcome.

The series of *Joie De Vivre* was crucial in Matisse's art. The completed work combined broad areas of pure, flat colour with sinuous arabesques to provide an idyllic setting for a harem of western women. This earthly paradise looked back to Renaissance paintings such as Titian's *The Andrians* of 1520 or, more recently, Ingres' *The*

Age Of Gold, but it used oriental motifs in a way Matisse was to make his own, most notably in his *Odalisque* series (page 20). Such secret, sensual paradises were to recur throughout the art of this essentially shy, reclusive man.

The Fauvist furore made Matisse famous. The Russian merchant Sergei Shchukin commissioned works like *Dance* (page 10) and *The Dinner Table* (page 12); perceptive Americans like the Steins began to buy his work. Such commissions transformed Matisse's finances and he began to travel - to Italy, Algeria, Russia, Spain and Germany, where he saw a huge Islamic exhibition at Munich in 1910.

1931: Matisse outlining sections of Dance in the Musée d'Art Moderne de la Ville de Paris

France, finally moving to Nice in 1916, living in various hotel suites. The brilliant colours and warmth of the south appealed deeply to him and are reflected in the sensual works he painted there - odalisques (pages 20 or 22; slave girls in oriental harems) or still lifes of glowing interiors (pages 16 or 28).

In 1925 he was made a Chevalier of the Legion d'Honneur - such public honours being a far cry from the fury over Fauvism. His life seemed to settle into a private idyll of "calme et volupté". In pursuit of this idyll, partly following Gauguin, he made a voyage across the Pacific in 1930, calling on Gauguin's son in Tahiti. By this time he was separated from his wife; a Russian model Lydia Delektoreskaya took her place in his affections in the 1930s and 1940s.

Then came the Second World War and the German occupation. His wife and son were arrested by the Gestapo; he himself underwent an operation for duodenal cancer in 1941 that left him permanently confined to a wheelchair. But this did not stop him working, for he felt he had been given a new lease of life, and he painted a last series of interiors such as *Large Red Interior* (page 28). Worried about the prospect of a naval bombardment of Nice, he moved inland to the small village of Vence. In gratitude to the nuns who had nursed him, he designed their Chapel of the Rosary at Vence in 1948, employing radically simple designs (page 3). He also embarked on another totally original form of art - *gouaches coupées,* brightly coloured paper cut-outs.

Further honours came with the Grand prize at the Venice Biennale in 1950 and then a major retrospective exhibition at the Museum of Modern Art in New York. He died on 3 November 1954 at Nice and was buried at Cimiez, not far from where the Musée Matisse now stands on the edge of Nice.

Matisse modelling the crucifix for the Chapel of the Convent at Vence

Matisse now tried to combine the flat, decorative elements of Islamic art with western figurative art. This combination is apparent in *Interior With Aubergines* (page 12) with its decorative pattern derived from an oriental carpet. He greatly admired the Moorish architecture of Granada during a visit in 1911. Although he had met Picasso in 1906, Matisse always remained sceptical of Cubism, whose rigours were inherently alien to his love of colour.

In 1910 Matisse moved into a large house in the suburbs of Paris at Issy-les-Moulineaux. He himself came to enjoy wintering in the south of

The Chapel at Vence: the altar, trhe Virgin and Child and part of the Stations of the Cross. The furnishings were a also designed by Matisse

STUDY FOR JOIE DE VIVRE

1905 - Oil on canvas, 46.5 x 53 cm
Copenhagen, National Museum for Art

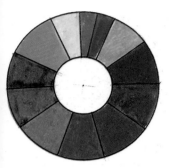

At the beginning of the description of each of the works which follow there is a revealing quotation by Matisse taken from his *Ecrits Sur L'Art* (Writings On Art) or from various interviews. As well as this, a circle of colours shows the colours chosen by Matisse for the work in question and indicates the relationship of proportions and tones. Matisse used to keep a colour circle for use in his studio. Its colours were arranged in the order of the spectrum: yellow, orange, red, violet, blue and green, with many gradations between one tone and the next.

This painting is also called *Landscape At Collioure*. Collioure was a small fishing village close to the Spanish border where Signac, the late Impressionist painter had settled. It was there, during the summer of 1905, Matisse and André Derain slowly evolved a new style, freeing themselves from the Pointillist ideas of Signac which had been so marked in Matisse's *Luxe, Calme Et Volupté* of the previous year. Matisse painted many landscapes around Collioure, fired by its brilliant Mediterranean colours. This is a study for the famous painting which epitomises the spirit of the Fauvists (wild beasts). Unfortunately, the Barnes Foundation does not permit colour reproductions of the finished work, to which Matisse added nudes scattered idyllically around the lansdscape

The style of this picture is deeply indebted to Gauguin's works, which had been much exhibited in the preceding two years. What distinguishes this painting, however, is its vibrant colours laid on with seeming abandon and its snaky, swirling forms. This combination struck contemporaries as utterly new.

Maurice Vlaminck: By The Edge Of The Seine At Carrières-Sur-Seine - 1906 - Oil on canvas, 54 x 65 cm - Private collection.
This painting by Vlaminck uses bright, flamboyant colours, as in the red of the branches which blaze across the sky and the river. Vlaminck described himself as "a tender barbarian filled with violence. I translated what I saw instinctively without any method, and conveyed truth not so much artistically as humanely." In this, he was more Fauvist than Matisse himself.

PORTRAIT WITH THE GREEN STRIPE

1905 - Oil on canvas, 40 x 32 cm
Copenhagen, National Museum for Art

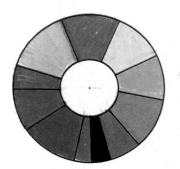

"Fauvism overthrew the tyranny of Divisionism (Pointillism). One can't live too long in a house well kept by country aunts. One must go off into the jungle to find simple ways that won't crush the spirit."

Portrait Of André Derain - 1905 - Oil on canvas, 38 x 28 cm - London, Tate Gallery. Another Fauvist portrait based on the interplay of strong colours, this time of Matisse's fellow artist Derain, whom many at the time considered a more promising painter. Derain's head is turned away from the spectator, with his main features drawn in tints of cobalt blue and green contrasting with the lurid red on one side of his head.

This was one of the most shockingly original works Matisse exhibited at the Salon d'Automne in 1905. There had been nothing in portraits by the Impressionists or Post-Impressionists to prepare the public for this portrait of the artist's wife (who often was his model in his early years) with an immense green stripe running down the centre of her face. There was something of the romantic rebels' desire to shock and startle in many of the first Fauvist paintings. As Matisse himself later said, "I overdid everything as a matter of course and worked by instinct with colour alone."

This was painted at the end of the summer of 1905 at Collioure, when Matisse was under the spell of Gauguin's Tahitian paintings. *The Green Stripe* had scarcely been finished when it was shown at the Salon d'Automne.

The traditional techniques of employing light and shadow to produce depth are here replaced by flat areas of contrasting colours. These form the background to a portrait of great psychological insight, far removed from most of Matisse's sensuous nudes of the period. The same techniques would have been much less startling in a landscape than in a portrait. Yet in its solid, almost sculptural power it is essentially closer to traditional painting than many Fauvist works.

These self-portraits of Matisse, 1939 - Pencil drawings - Philadelphia, Museum of Art - reveal another side of Matisse as a portraitist, showing him as a superb draughtsman as well as a great colourist. He appears almost as a Chinese sage. This is perhaps a suitable resemblance for a painter who had by this time long retired from the centre of art and artistic life to cultivate his own "inner paradise" at Nice. Matisse here painted himself in four different attitudes; not only does his expression change markedly from drawing to drawing, but the very shape of his chin and head seems to alter, without in any way ceasing to be a self-portrait.

INTERIOR WITH AUBERGINES

1911/12 - Mixed medium on canvas, 210 x 245 cm Grenoble, Musée de Peinture et de Sculpture

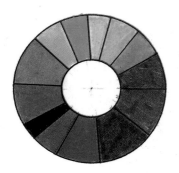

" **J**ewels and arabesques never overcrowd my drawings, compared with the object depicted, because these jewels and arabesques are an integral part of my picture. When well placed, they suggest the form or emphasis necessary to the composition of the drawing."

This is one of the four "symphonic interiors" (again Matisse used a musical expression to describe his work) which shows Matisse's family, studio or his rooms at Collioure transformed into gigantic schemes to be decorations. In fact, they were never hung together. This was the only one of the paintings actually executed at Collioure in southern France.

Despite the removal of a floral border about 18 cm wide around it, this is also the largest and most decorative of the four interiors. Its matt surface was painted in a mixed medium which produced a nearly fresco-like effect, recalling that used for *Luxe, Calme Et Volupté* (Luxury, Calm, Delight - lines taken from a poem by Baudelaire) seven years earlier.

A green screen has been placed right in the centre of the painting to help the colours overlap.

The original floral border which he removed (for reasons not known) would have made the painting resemble an eastern carpet even more closely. Besides acting as a pattern, the floral motif suggests a profusion of flowers in a luxuriant garden paradise.

The Islamic influence is obvious. From 1911, Matisse made several trips to Morocco. He had admired Islamic art for a long time and its influence can be traced in the

arabesques which are typical of his work from 1911-14. The importance of patterns in Islamic art comes from the religious instruction not to show figures in any graven form. Although semi-recognisable figures are found, the profusion of motifs and patterns are a compensation for lack of form. Matisse found his stays in Morocco restoring and inspiring. "I found the landscape of Morocco just as they had been described in the paintings of Delacroix...One morning in Tangier I was riding in a meadow; the flowers came up the horse's muzzle."

Like Gauguin, Matisse here wished to use pure colour in independent large blocks.

The Dinner Table - *Oil on canvas - 180 x 220 cm - Leningrad, Hermitage Museum. This painting hung among the 15 Gauguins in Shchukin's dining-room in Moscow. It was started in the spring of 1908 with a blue background and was modified the following year in favour of a harmony of reds. It is therefore one of the most thought-out of the artist's works, in which Fauvist experimentation co-exists with his theories about colour.*

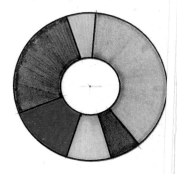

PIANO LESS

This painting, e
darkest days of
shows Matisse
and least colou
time when he c
intellectual rig
before rejectir
of colour and
This is certainl
most disciplin
(architectural
son Pierre wa:
piano of the M
les-Moulineau
surrogate for
keenly intere:
Matisse's own
A High Stool,
the wall behir
sculptures, *D*
the bottom le
such domesti
unusually so
The garden,
window on t
single triang
of grey fill n
space, apart
piano itself i
the piano, th
marks the b
a nearly abs

ODALISQUE WITH A TAMBOURINE

1926 - Oil on canvas, 73 x 54 cm -
New York, Private collection

"Thick paint does not give out light, it is the combination of light which is wanted. For instance, do not try to strengthen your forms with intense light. Much better to support them by the way they interrelate. Red must be used to give depth to blue and yellow. But put it where it is useful ... in the background perhaps."

After the First World War when he moved to Nice for the greater part of the year, Matisse returned to painting in the more elegant and colourful style which he preferred. His series of *Odalisques* was created in a rather self-consciously sumptuous atmosphere. At first Matisse lived in hotel rooms but in 1921 he rented the former apartment of Frank Harris, the English writer, at Place Charles-Felix, sited at the bottom of the castle hill and gardens of Nice. Here he began to change the way he painted nudes. Instead of painting them as simple girls posing unaffectedly, he began to cast them as oriental odalisques (girls in harems) acting out dreams of luxury and calm, delighting in his theatrical settings. Often he painted them wearing harem trousers. This painting is relatively restrained and straightforward. Here Matisse concentrated on the volume of the female nude reclining in her armchair with the contours of her body hightlighted by the bright light. The colours are dominated by the brilliant red of the floor and the strong green and yellow striped chair. The nude stands out against the harmony of the light and shade of the reflected colours. Outside the window, the blue southern sky gleams brilliantly down again.

The sketch illustrates the way in which the classical pose of the model, with her arm around her head, and the construction of the figure seem to relate to Matisse's idea that one must "set the pieces of the figure firmly into each other, assembling them as a carpenter builds a house."

Nude Study - 1935 - Pen and Ink - New York, Private collection. This very fine drawing dates from the middle of Matisse's so-called Classical decade of the 1930s, when he returned to classical forms for inspiration. The mirror which reflects his young model and reveals her back and sides finds a humorous echo in the easel and pen of the artist in the right foreground.

LARGE RED INTERIOR

1948 - Oil on canvas, 126 x 89 cm
Paris, Centre Georges Pompidou

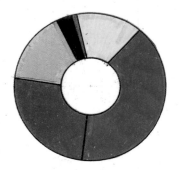

"*An artist must possess Nature. He must identify himself with her rhythm, through efforts which prepare him for that mastery by which he will later be able to express himself in his own language and style.*"

This is the last of Matisse's final great series of oil paintings, begun in 1947 before increasing ill-health led him to concentrate almost exclusively on his *gouaches coupées* (paper cut-outs) and drawings to illustrate books. He said that he saw these *Interiors* as having "through reduced means all the qualities of a painting or a mural." This included *Interior With Egyptian Curtain* and *The Lived-In Silence Of Houses* (below).

Large Red Interior was particularly significant because of its red, which had always been one of his favourite colours. The overall tone is far more muted here, however, than in earlier works such as *Dance*, (page 10). The monochromatic expanse of red induces a serious rather than a joyous mood.

But there are still playful touches: an animal skin, presumably of a bear, seems to pursue that of a leopard across the floor and then it recurs in his painting *The Pineapple* which is seen hanging above the table. Matisse again features his own works in his painting; *Interior With Window And Palm* hangs opposite. The general white ground (base) of the canvas is left exposed in various places to evoke some feeling of light. This is a markedly two-dimensional, almost flat, canvas.

After this Matisse gave up painting in oils. Although now in his late seventies, he turned to new, simpler forms of art and the gouaches coupées were born. He also used very simple clean lines in his designs for architecture and murals of the Chapel at Vence.

The Lived-In Silence Of Houses - 1947 - Oil on canvas - 61 x 50 cm - Paris, Private collection. The mood in this picture is generally melancholy, with its figures being nearly absorbed into the surrounding black. Only in the landscape beyond the window is there any real colour or joy. Matisse has scratched a graffito-like signature into the top left-hand corner.

The sketch illustrates again the basic simplicity of the composition: it is based on the crossing of the two central axes, which mark out the four parts of the picture containing the four principal motifs, linked by a single element: the chair.

Matisse was very explicit and forthcoming about his attitudes to painting - remarkably so for an essentially shy, reserved man. In *Notes Of A Painter* of 1908, he attempted to state the basis of his art just when he was in the full flood of his own artistic development. Although accepting that "a painter's best spokesman is his work", he was willing to write about art, as Ingres and Delacroix, had done before.

Matisse by 1908 was 39, no longer a young man and, although his art would still develop and change in many ways, he never effectively shifted from the opinions he then expressed. Matisse wrote of his "almost religious awe towards life"; he clearly had a nearly religious belief in art also.

The artist, he thought, worked towards an ideal which he intuitively understood, being especially finely-tuned to translate his perceptions of nature into art. Matisse was not concerned with the argument over the rival claims of nature or the imagination as the true source of art; both he saw as vital. Artists, he said, whilst realising that their pictures were artificial, should feel they were copying nature when producing a painting.

He felt that Giotto, whose superb frescoes in the Arena Chapel at Padua he had seen in 1907, stood at one end of the Western artistic tradition, and Cézanne, his great hero, at the other. Matisse, as an impoverished unknown, had bought Cézanne's *The Three Bathers* in 1899. Although Cézanne is generally considered the greatest Post-Impressionist, Matisse significantly saw him more as a classical artist and so the true heir of Poussin, who is accepted as the greatest of all French classical painters. "What I dream of," wrote Matisse, "is an art of balance, purity and serenity, de-

MATISSE AND HIS TIMES

	HIS LIFE AND WORKS	HISTORY	ART AND CULTURE
1869	Born 31 December at Le Cateau in northern France	Birth of Gandhi Opening of the Suez Canal Irish Disestablishment Act disestablishes the (Anglican) church in Ireland	Gustave Flaubert: *Sentimental Education* John Stuart Mill: *The Subjugation Of Women* Tolstoy: *War And Peace*
1890	While convalescing from appendicitis, he starts to paint to pass the time	Dismissal of Bismarck as Chancellor of Germany Parnall Scandal damages Irish Nationalist cause	Debussy sets *Five Poems* by Baudelaire to music Oscar Wilde: *The Picture Of Dorian Grey* Van Gogh commits suicide
1891	He moves to Paris, where he enters first the Académie Julien, then the Académie des Beaux-Arts	Creation of the Pangermanist Union reflects growing German nationalism. Michelin invents the pneumatic tyre	Thomas Hardy: *Tess Of The D'Urbevilles* Gauguin: *On The Beach* Gaudi building Barcelona Cathedral
1897	His *Woman Reading* is bought by the state; he seems set on a career of conventional success	Queen Victoria's Golden Jubilee Diesel invents his diesel engine	Bram Stoker: *Dracula* Chekhov: *Uncle Vanya* W.B. Yeats: *The Secret Rose*
1899	He meets André Derain. Birth of his second child Jean	Outbreak of the Boer War; many British defeats Rehabilitation of Dreyfus in France	Edward Elgar: *Enigma Variations* W.B. Yeats: *The Wind In The Reeds* Alfred Jarry: *Père Ubu*
1900	Birth of his third and last child, Pierre. By this time he is painting in an experimental but commercially unsuccessful way	World Fair in Paris Zeppelin makes first flight in airship Relief of Mafeking after long siege in South Africa	Toulouse-Lautrec: *The Modiste* Colette: *Claudine At School* Joseph Conrad: *Lord Jim*
1901	He meets Maurice Vlaminck and exhibits at the Salon des Indépendants, which is presided over by the Pointillist Signac	Death of Queen Victoria in Britain; Edward VII succeeds her Assassination of President McKinley; Theodore Roosevelt succeeds him	Thomas Mann: *Buddenbroks* Death of Toulouse-Lautrec Rudyard Kipling: *Kim*
1904	First exhibition at Vollards. At Saint Tropez with Signac he experiments with Pointillism, painting *Luxe, Calme Et Volupté*	Anglo-French Entente Cordiale formed against Germany Outbreak of Russo-Japanese War	Chekhov: *The Cherry Orchard* Cézanne: *Montagne Sainte Victoire*
1905	Exhibition at the Salon d'Automne with Vlaminck, Derain and others causes a scandal; Gertrude Stein buys *Woman With A Hat*	Destruction of Russian fleet by Japanese First Revolution in Russia after Bloody Sunday in St Petersburg Norway gains independence	Birth of Anthony Powell and Kenneth Clarke Picasso: *The Saltimbanques* Cézanne: *The Bathers*

void of troubling or depressing subject matter."

These *Notes Of A Painter,* swiftly translated into several foreign languages, were at odds with his image as "king of the Fauvists"(wild men). But Matisse had never relished such a title and was happy to drop it as soon as he could. Fauvism, he later said, "was for me an experiment with ways of painting, juxtaposing and contrasting expressively reds, blues and greens. It derived from a need I felt within me and not from any voluntary or rational attitude."

Matisse had opened a school in 1904 to supplement his income from painting. The following year, the notoriety following the exhibition at the Salon d'Automne began to make his name known as much abroad as in France, which boosted his school. By 1911 it was attracting so many students from Europe and America, that it was interfering with his work and he gave it up.

Patrons, notably Russians like Shchukin, one of the most perceptive men of his age, now ordered enough commissions, for works like *The Dance* or *The Dinner Table,* for Matisse to live comfortably. Americans like Gertrude Stein were also now buying his works. Indeed, Matisse was first fully recognised by foreigners, not Frenchmen.

By 1911 Matisse could hardly have been regarded as an obvious rebel in any sense. He seemed to be living a bourgeois life in his large suburban house, with his wife, children and daily routine. Further, his style and palette had cooled from the violence which had astounded the world at the Salon d'Automne in 1905. Unlike his friend and former colleague Maurice Vlaminck, a fervent anarchist in politics who long remained devoted to Fauvist ideals, Matisse's art had already moved on towards

1907	Travels to Italy for the first time, where he is overwhelmed by Giotto's works. Paints *Nude In Blue*	Rasputin establishes dominance over the Imperial Russian court New Zealand becomes a self-governing dominion	Birth of W.H. Auden Kipling wins the Nobel Prize for Literature James Joyce: *Chamber Music* Picasso: *Les Demoiselles D'Avignon*
1911	Visits Morocco for the first time. Paints *Goldfish And Sculpture,* starts *Interior With Aubergines*	Parliament Act in Britain reduces powers of the House of Lords Italy starts conquest of Libya Amundsen beats Scott to South Pole	Richard Strauss: *The Rosenkavalier* Max Beerbohm: *Zuleika Dobson* Lutyens builds Castle Drogo
1916	His paintings become more austere and geometrical; paints *Piano Lesson.* Starts spending the winters in Nice	Battles of Verdun and the Somme Lloyd George becomes Prime Minister British use tanks for the first time German fleet defeated at Battle of Jutland	Sigmund Freud: *Introduction to Psychoanalysis* Death of Henry James Franz Kafka: *Metamorphosis*
1918	Finishes *Interior With A Violin.* Exhibits in Paris with Picasso	Collapse of Germany and Austria; end of the First World War	Lytton Strachey: *Eminent Victorians* James Joyce: *Exiles* Guillaume Apollinaire: *Calligrammes*
1937	Designs the set for Shostakovitch's ballet *The Red And The Black;* paints *Lady In Blue*	Chamberlain becomes Prime Minister Coronation of George VI Japanese attempt conquest of China	W.H. Auden and Louis Macniece: *Letters From Iceland* Picasso: *Guernica*
1944	Moves to Vence, to escape attacks on Nice. His wife and son arrested by the Gestapo	Allied landings in Normandy Von Stauffenberg plot against Hitler fails	Death of Edwin Lutyens Jean-Paul Sartre: *Huis Clos*
1948	Starts the decorations for the Chapel of the Rosary at Vence. Paints *Large Red Interior*	Gandhi assassinated by Hindu fanatic Berlin Airlift started to beat Russian blockade of Berlin	Graham Greene: *The Heart Of The Matter* W.B. Yeats: *Collected Poems (post)*
1950	Wins the Grand Prix at the Venice Biennale	Start of the Korean War Britain recognises Communist government of China China invades Tibet	Eugene Ionesco: *The Bald Prima Donna* Stanley Spencer: *Resurrection: Port Glasgow*
1954	Dies at Nice November 3	French defeat at Dien Bien Phu ends French rule in Vietnam; Vietnam divided Nasser becomes President of Egypt Roger Bannister becomes first man to run the mile in 4 minutes	Kingsley Amis: *Lucky Jim* Anthony Burgess: *St Venus' Eve* T.S. Eliot: *The Confidential Clerk*

creating an enclosed world of beauty and calm, almost like the world of an imaginary harem.

In this respect he was utterly different from Picasso, who seemed exuberantly to lead or to join almost every art movement in the first half of the century. There was to be nothing like Picasso's famous denunciation of war *Guernica,* painted in 1937 in Matisse's art. Indeed, during the Second World War, while his wife and son were both arrested by the Gestapo and deported, he continued to paint unhurriedly, seemingly detached from outer worries. But such detachment, perhaps the key to his mature art, had been attained no more easily than his seemingly simple pictures, each of which he reworked constantly.

THE IMPACT OF ISLAM

In 1911 Matisse and his wife made their first, prolonged trip to Morocco. Its colours were a revelation to Matisse as they had been over 80 years earlier to Delacroix, the great Romantic painter. This impact - reinforced by a second trip the following year - helped to buttress Matisse's own art against the rival claims of Cubism, of which by this time he was very much aware. *Interior With Aubergines* (page 12) reveals the influence of Islamic art in its brilliant colours and geometric, flat patterns derived from carpets. He had seen and been vastly impressed by the huge Islamic Art Exhibition at Munich in 1910. In Islamic art prohibitions on depicting the human form had led instead to elaborate, often geometric, two-dimensional forms. In *Dance* this flattening of form was very evident.

The Piano Lesson (page 14), painted in 1916 - one of the grimmest years of the First World War - is one of Matisse's most restrained paintings. It shows his closest confrontation with Cubism. Yet he was to paint no more in this austere and monochromatic vein. That year Matisse began to avoid the grey winters of Paris by spending them in Nice, whose bright colours and subtropical flowers appealed to him greatly; increasingly, he also turned away from the art world of Paris, seemingly happy to leave to Picasso leadership of the avant-garde.

THE INNER PARADISE

The 11 years that followed Matisse's final move to Nice in 1918 have been called his Impressionist years. As with the Impressionists, the light of the Côte d'Azur played a major role in his paintings; so too did the Impressionists' concern with domesticity, interiors and what gives pleasure in art. In this Matisse was echoing the concerns of his friend Pierre Bonnard along the coast at Le Cannet, but with the difference that Matisse had experimented far more deeply and widely. Matisse was only one of many French painters who turned south (Renoir, Signac, Bonnard and later even Picasso also did so). "If I had gone on painting up north, my painting would have been different," he told the poet Louis Aragon in 1942. "There would have been cloudiness, greys, colours, shading off in the distance."

His *Interior With A Violin*, probably begun in Paris but certainly finished in Nice in 1918, marks the beginnings of this new strength of colour. The blinding heat of the Mediterranean gleams through the shutters into a shaded, secretive interior. This Matisse soon filled with the voluptuous women (recurrent through his works) like *Odalisque With The Tambourine* (1926).

In the 1930s Matisse, now very successful commercially, received a commission from the American millionaire Dr Barnes. Barnes had built up a great collection of modern art and Matisse agreed to paint murals on the vaults of his private museum at Merion. He chose the theme of the dance again, and his huge, simple white forms against blocks of colour revealed his neo-classical style in its maturity.

After his recovery from an operation for duodenal cancer in 1941, Matisse, instead of continuing contentedly with the same styles which had made him famous and fairly rich, felt that he had to exploit this new lease of life. He struck out yet again in new directions, although confined to a wheelchair. Illustrations for poems - brilliantly simple drawings - remained one of his favoured media in these last 13 years of his life, but the same simplicity of design was apparent on a much larger scale in his famous murals and designs for the Chapel of the Rosary at Vence (page 2).

He still also painted the occasional superb interior, such as *Large Red Interior*. But he concentrated after the war mainly on his gouaches- coupées (paper cut-outs), which he literally cut out, painted and then pinned to the wall or canvas. Of these the most famous is the beautifully-coloured, nearly abstract, *Sorrows Of The King*. In these simple bright colours and shapes, the immobilised Matisse seemed to rediscover some of the joys of childhood's imagination. One or two critics questioned the value of these last, most original, works, but not Picasso. When he heard of his great rival's death in 1954, the Spanish painter said, "Yes, he is dead and I am left to continue his work."

With the revival of interest in figurative art in recent years, and the corresponding decline in the reputation of abstract art, Matisse's treatment of the human figure between the wars has come to be seen as important as his dramatic use of colour at the beginning and end of his career. In his depiction of the human form, Matisse showed that he was indeed the heir of the French classical tradition, from Poussin to Cézanne, and not le Fauve (the wild man) his early critics and enthusiasts had proclaimed him. But his was a classicism which had confronted, and then managed to rise above, the most severe challenges of the Modern Movement, especially Cubism, to create its own inner paradise.